How to Change the World

Change Management 3.0

Jurgen Appelo

www.management30.com/how-to-change-the-world

Rotterdam, The Netherlands

jojo@noop.nl

How to Change the World : Change Management 3.0 / Jurgen Appelo

ISBN 978-90-819051-1-4

Version 1.01 – May 2012

Contents

Foreword

It's no secret that the world is in need of change. As we look around our little planet, we see that the human race has managed to create a set of organizations that increasingly dispirit the people who are doing the work and frustrate the people for whom the work is being done. Young people entering the workplace increasingly see a world that is hollow and empty of real meaning.

Even on their own terms, our organizations are failing. Despite the confident pronouncements of today's leaders, studies show that our organizations are much less productive than they once were and going out of business faster and faster [Denning 2012a]. The ways in which we got things done in the 20th Century are no longer working for us [Denning 2012b].

Equally, the ways in which we made change happen in the 20th Century are also failing. The top-down authority-riddled eight-step change programs that were once deployed no longer have the credibility to generate a genuine sense of urgency or a meaningful version of the future of which people really want to be part.

Fortunately, Jurgen Appelo has written this helpful handbook on how to make change happen in our emerging world. It's about sparking change that engages people hearts as well as minds. It's about change that draws on everyone's talents and creativity, not just the schemes of a few experts at the top.

Instead of articulating a top-down vision to be rolled out from above, crushing "obstacles" in its path, it's about inviting people to dance with complexity. Instead of mining "human resources", it's about minding the people. Instead of tending the vertical hierarchy, it's about stimulating the horizontal network. Instead of constructing firewalls to insulate the firm from its context, it's about engaging with the environment.

Getting started in the right way is usually the hardest and most important step. Reasons and arguments don't work: they just lead to counter-arguments and more arguments. Instead, the best way to begin is to find an example of things going well somewhere, and then to communicate that in a story. By getting people to talk in a story-telling mode about times when things went well, they come up with their own ideas that contain the kernel of the future.

The sensible steps described in this handbook were not dreamed up in some academic ivory tower. They are the hard-won product of many failures. Jurgen is almost a connoisseur of failure: he charmingly describes how he was a failure for more than fifteen years before finding more productive paths. Happily he has decided to share with us what he learned in his journey.

The challenge is bigger and tougher than we think. When the building blocks of society are broken, it's not just a matter of working harder or finding a quick fix. It's about dreaming large ideas and thinking, speaking and acting differently. It's about persisting when the odds seem impossible. It goes beyond fiddling at the margin. It requires inspiring deep change that entails unlearning most of what we know for sure, things that are taught in every business school and assumed as fundamental truths in most management textbooks.

Woven throughout the handbook is the story of the Stoos gathering, of which I was privileged to be a part. Twenty-one people came together in January 2012 in a tiny village in the mountains of Switzerland with the absurd idea of creating a common banner under which many people intent on changing organizations around the world might join hands and march together to create a better future. We had no idea whether anyone would note or remember what we came up with. By practicing the principles described in this handbook, within a month our little group had grown to more than six hundred.

Of course, this is just a beginning. Much remains to be accomplished. The challenge is immense and will require the participation of millions. But like Margaret Mead, we have never doubted that a small group of thoughtful, committed citizens could change the world. Indeed, it is the only thing that ever has.

Stephen Denning
Author of *The Leader's Guide to Radical Management* and
The Leader's Guide to Storytelling.

Acknowledgements

This is a very small book and I should try to keep the size of this section proportional to the remainder of this work. But I can't. My gratitude toward those who helped me, either knowingly or unknowingly, is as large as always.

Thanks to the people who attend my courses and my talks at conferences. I always enjoy good discussions and feedback, and I wouldn't have been able to write this text without your stories.

Thanks to the active people in the Agile Lean Europe network. I am so proud that you've turned a simple idea into reality, and I'm thankful that this triggered and enabled me to learn a lot about change management.

Thanks to the participants in the Stoos Network. It is great to converse and collaborate with people who are passionate about the same things as I am.

Thanks to Steve Denning for agreeing to write a wonderful foreword for this little book.

Thanks to the reviewers: Alyssa Fox, Andrea Chiou, Ángel Medinilla, Anne Schüßler, Arne Åhlander, Christine Koppelt, Christof Braun, Deb Hartmann Preuss, Erwin van der Koogh, Ewan O'Leary, Gitte Klitgaard Hansen, Jürgen de Smet, Lisa Crispin, Maarten Volders, Marcin Floryan, Mischa Ramseyer, Nina Kaurel, Peter Stevens, Rudie de Bruin, Saket Bivalkar, Ted M. Young, Voranc Kutnik, Yves Ferland, and Yves Stalgies. Together you've saved me from a lot of embarrassment.

Thanks to Nadira Rambocus, Erik Gille, Linda Hirzmann and Mick Schouten. It's great to call you my "team members" when I'm on the other side of the planet.

And thank you, blog readers, Twitter followers, Facebook friends, and book readers. You still keep me going. Don't stop!

If this booklet is a success then next time I might thank myself.

About the Author

Jurgen Appelo is a writer, speaker, trainer, entrepreneur, illustrator, developer, manager, blogger, reader, dreamer, leader, freethinker, and… Dutch guy.

Since 2008 Jurgen writes a popular blog at NOOP.NL, that covers topics including Agile management, software engineering, business improvement, personal development, and complexity theory. He is the author of the book *Management 3.0: Leading Agile Developers, Developing Agile Leaders*, which describes the role of the manager in Agile organizations. He is also a speaker who is regularly invited to talk at business seminars and conferences around the world.

After studying Software Engineering at the Delft University of Technology, and earning his Master's degree in 1994, Jurgen Appelo has busied himself starting up and leading a variety of Dutch businesses, always in the position of team leader, manager, or executive. Jurgen has experience in leading a horde of 100 software developers, development managers, project managers, business consultants, quality managers, service managers, and kangaroos, some of which he hired accidentally.

Nowadays he works full-time developing innovative courseware, books, and other types of original content. But sometimes Jurgen puts it all aside to spend time on his ever-growing collection of science fiction and fantasy literature, which he stacks in a self-designed book case. It is 4 meters high.

Jurgen lives in Rotterdam (The Netherlands) -- and in Brussels (Belgium) -- with his partner Raoul. He has two kids, and an imaginary hamster called George.

jurgenappelo.com

management30.com

noop.nl

Preface

It is one of the questions I get most often: How do I deal with my crappy organization? I like my work but I don't like what our management is doing. How do I deal with it?

Well, that's easy. You have three options:

1. Ignore it. Changing organizations is hard work. If you don't have the stamina to learn how to be a good change agent, then stop complaining about what's bad. Accept that the organization is what it is, and enjoy the good parts of your work. In that case, you can stop reading here.

2. Quit your job. The only reason there are bad organizations is that people don't quit their jobs. Do the world a favor and find a better place to work. Help bad organizations out of their misery by not working for them.

3. Learn about change management. Most people are terrible at influencing other people and changing organizations. But, if you're serious about it, you can learn how to be a more effective change agent.

As my friend Olaf Lewitz said, "It's take it, leave it, or change it…"

I wrote this booklet for those who choose option 3.

Jurgen Appelo

Rotterdam, March 2012

jurgen@noop.nl

From Failure to Furor

I haven't the slightest idea how to change people,
but I still keep a long list of prospective candidates just in case I should ever figure it out.

David Sedaris, American writer (1956)

W. Edwards Deming wrote decades ago that bonuses are bad for business [Deming 1986]. But most managers around the world are still using them. Peter F. Drucker said ages ago that knowledge workers cannot be subordinates of managers [Drucker 1974], but managers still act as if they are other people's superiors. And research tells us again and again that performance appraisals don't work [Bobinski 2010]. But many managers keep relying on them as their primary evaluation technique.

Why?

Why is management changing so slowly (or not at all)?

The Agile Manifesto[1] has made a big impact on software development around the world in a matter of 10 years. Granted, we're not done yet. But we've made significant progress. However, it seems the Arctic Ocean will have melted before we see traditional management being replaced with a new paradigm.

Ideas for improving organizations have been around for decades. And yet, very little has happened. Change in business management is happening at a glacial pace. Can we help accelerate the transformation of the way organizations are run? Can we heat things up? Can we energize the movement for global change?

Together with many other management thinkers and practitioners I am looking for ideas on how to energize a global movement for

[1] Agile Manifesto, http://agilemanifesto.org/

organizational transformation. That means change management of epic proportions, on a global scale. Ambitious? Yes. Difficult? Certainly. Possible? I don't know. But at least it keeps me off the streets.

In this booklet I will discuss an approach to change management that has proven to work on smaller scales. It *might* also work on a global scale. It *could* help you in your attempt at changing your organization. But it *definitely* helped me at changing mine.

But before we will see where it takes us, I will tell you about the many times I was *not* able to change my environment.

15 Years of Failure

I love bragging about the fact that I have been a failure for more than 15 years. In 1992 I tried to start an international newsletter about dance music, and I failed. In 1994 I tried to launch a game development company, and I failed. I spent three years writing bookkeeping software, but I sold it to only a few customers. In 1997, with a friend, I started a software company, which was successful for a while. But eventually, together with the parent company, it collapsed. (Just like the dozen or so relationships I had in that decade.)

The first signs of change seemed to arrive in 1999, when I launched an Internet startup that produced games charts. My business plan was so impressive that I won a national award for it. And it helped to attract one million euros from informal investors. My team and I were quite successful at *spending* all that money to the last euro. But, alas, we didn't find any customers, and this business collapsed as well. I will spare you my many failures between 2000 and 2008, which included a novel, a cartoon, a blog, another book, and several original but doomed software projects. Again and again I tried to have some impact on the world around me. And every time I failed.

Did I give up? Of course not.

Starting in 2008, for some inexplicable reasons, things changed. My blog NOOP.NL is a success, hailed as the 3rd most popular Agile blog in the world [Saddington 2010]. My book *Management 3.0*[2] is a success,

---

[2] Management 3.0, http://www.management30.com/

generating lots of invites for seminars and conferences. My course seems to be a success, earning excellent evaluations all over the world. My latest relationship fared well enough that we decided to get married. And my idea to start the *Agile Lean Europe network*[3] resulted in *ALE 2011*[4], an amazing pan-European conference in Berlin, with more than 200 attendees.

Sometimes people ask me, "What has changed?" or "How did you do that?"

Indeed, I've been wondering about that too...

Maybe I have exhausted the total supply of failure that was available for me in the universe. Maybe some god up there shook his head and said, "That's enough failure for you. If you go on like this there will be nothing left for the European government."

The only thing I can say with certainty is, I now spend much more time *learning* how to be a better writer, a better speaker, a better trainer. And a better change agent. It seems to be paying off.

Whatever the reasons, after so many failed attempts at making my ideas work, I picked up a thing or two about being a *somewhat successful* but certainly *very persistent* change agent. In this booklet I am going to tell you about the lessons I learned. And I hope it helps you to learn more quickly than I did.

How to Change Other People

The hardest part of continuous improvement in organizations is changing the behavior of *other* people. (At least, that's what people keep telling me.) When people want to be more professional knowledge workers, or have a more sustainable work environment, or a job that they actually enjoy, their organizations (the systems around the people) don't always co-operate. How do you "make" management more agile? How can you convince team members to educate themselves better? How can you influence colleagues to cooperate instead of competing? How can you steer customers so they pursue fair contracts and collaboration?

---

[3] ALE Network, http://alenetwork.eu/

[4] ALE 2011, http://ale2011.eu/

I have realized that all these challenges boil down to the same question:

> How do I change other people's behaviors?
> I know what they should be doing, but they're not doing it!

Christof Braun, Scrum consultant in Frankfurt, Germany

Is behavior really what you want to change? Don't you want to make them understand first? Change their value systems, and their beliefs? If you succeed at changing mindsets, people will behave differently and this may well lead to behaviors you had not expected but that could be even better than what you were hoping for.

It turns out that we are talking about basic *change management*. We all want to know **how to change a complex social system**. Or how to change the world. It's like politics, but without the bodyguards.

Luckily, there are lots of books available on this topic. *Switch* [Heath 2010], *Fearless Change* [Manns, Rising, 2005], *Leading Change* [Kotter, 1996], *Influencer* [Patterson 2008], and many others offer hundreds of pages full of useful advice for change agents. However, although some of these books are very good, most of them paint simplified pictures of change in social systems.

Complexity Thinking

Simple models, supported by inspiring stories, are good to get you started with the basics of change management. The real world, however, is far more complex than what most models would have you believe. We need a more complete approach to organizational change. It is very hard to predict how a complex social system will behave. We need to understand how to influence the whole system by poking at it. Then we see how it responds. As change agents we try to nudge people, teams and organizations so that they will reorganize themselves.

> "
> The trick, as with all the behavioral possibilities of complex systems, is to recognize what structures contain which latent behaviors, and what conditions release those behaviors - and, where possible, to arrange the structures and conditions to reduce the probability of destructive behaviors and to encourage the possibility of beneficial ones.
>
> - Donella H. Meadows, *Thinking in Systems* [Meadows 2008]

Smart people say, "You cannot make people behave differently." True, but while we can also not "make someone laugh" or "make someone happy", the least we can do is *try*. That is what change management is all about. Give it your best shot. But, whenever you can, make that shot a bit smarter than just an educated guess.

The Mojito Method

Many times I have communicated, on my blog and in my book, that I don't drink beer, wine, or other alcoholic drinks, with the exception of mojitos. I do this in the hope that, one day, I will be surprised by the spontaneous arrival of a fresh mojito in my hotel room. Regrettably, I have never been so fortunate. I'm an optimist, thought, so I won't give up hoping.

One thing I find fascinating about mojitos is that the taste is so amazing, despite the fact that the separate ingredients are actually rather boring. And I have noticed the same can also apply to ideas. When you mix different ideas from multiple sources, a new idea can emerge that both aggregates and improves on the pre-existing ideas.

I call it the **Mojito Method**.

My friends tell me I make excellent mojitos. I'm also quite skilled at applying the Mojito Method. I take ideas from other people, stir them up, and use them in a way that is even more useful than any of the ideas taken separately (I think). I describe the reason this can work in my own book:

> Recent research has shown that the copying of ideas is the most successful of all [improvement] strategies. [...] This would indicate that teams should spend most of their (learning) time copying ideas from other sources. Only a little time should be spent on inventing their own.
>
> - Jurgen Appelo, *Management 3.0* [Appelo 2011a]

The Mojito Method makes sense for anyone who wants to innovate without the trouble of inventing entirely new stuff. I did it with the *Happiness Door* (a combination of a *feedback wall* and a *happiness index*), with *Delegation Poker* (a mix of *servant leadership*, *key decision areas*, and *planning poker*), and with *Moving Motivators* (adapted from *16 Basic Desires* [Reiss 2002] and *Self-Determination Theory* [Deci, Ryan 2002]). [Appelo 2011b] [Appelo 2011c] [Appelo 2011d]

Now I intend to apply the Mojito Method to change management. Let's see if I can help you to crush resistance to change, and stir things up a little…

Change Management 3.0

No matter how big the CEO's chair is, an organization is not a machine driven by an owner. It is a social network. People interact with each other across all levels in the corporate hierarchy. While delivering a product or service is quite different from handing over the butter at the lunch table, while you chit-chat about the weekend, both involve social networks.

> We believe [...] that organizations can become learning networks of [diverse] individuals creating value.
>
> - Stoos Gathering communiqué[5]

[5] Stoos Network, http://www.stoosnetwork.org/

When you want to change behaviors in something as complex as a social system, you have to understand the four aspects of change management.

First, Dance with the System

A social network is *complex* and *adaptive* [Mitchell 2009]. It will adapt to your actions, and so you must adapt to the network. It is like dancing with a system. A complexity thinker understands that change rarely follows a straight path, and usually involves some bruised toes and elbows.

Second, Mind the People

Understand that people are the crucial parts of the social system, and that people are different. There's no one-approach-fits-all. And just asking people to change is rarely enough. Diversity is what makes complex systems work, and thus a *diversity of methods* is crucial when dealing with people.

Third, Stimulate the Network

Understand how behavior spreads through a complex system. In a social network it is all about individuals and their interactions. Behaviors spread like viruses, and *social network stimulation* can help overcome resistance to change and transform an entire organization.

Fourth, Change the Environment

People always organize themselves within the context of an environment. The environment determines how the system can self-organize, and you may be able to tweak the environment. Because people's behaviors depend on their environment, if you *change the environment* you change the people.

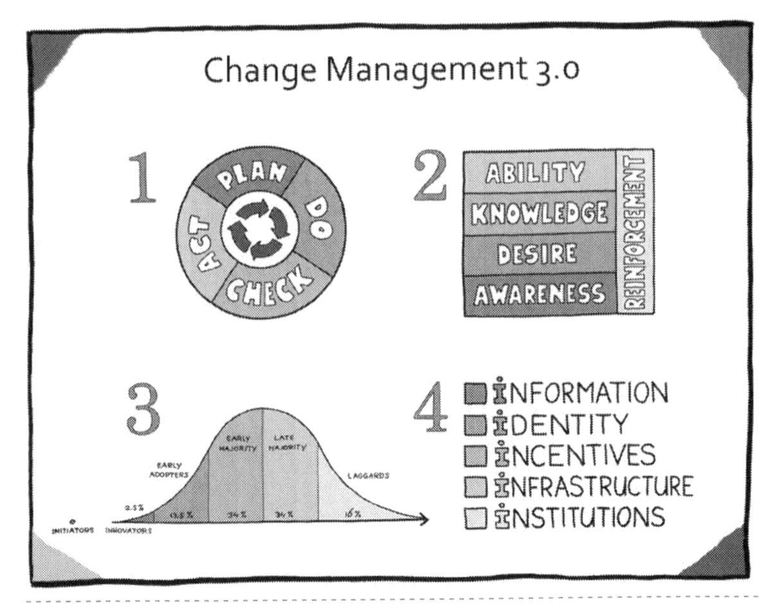

FIGURE 1: The four aspects of Change Management 3.0

The Change Management 3.0 Supermodel

If you understand these aspects of change management: Congratulations, you can apply the Change Management 3.0 *supermodel* (FIGURE 1). I call it a supermodel because it wraps a few smaller well-known models for change each addressing one of the four aspects I just outlined. It is the Mojito Method applied to change management.

1. **Dance with the System** - using the *PDCA* model

2. **Mind the People** - using the *ADKAR* model

3. **Stimulate the Network** - using the *Adoption Curve* model

4. **Change the Environment** - using the *Five I's* model

I describe each of the four smaller models in the next four chapters. Once you understand the supermodel you will be in a good position to try and "make" people more agile, better educated, more cooperative, or (if you like a good challenge) more willing to attend a performance of your choir.

Dance with the System

It is important that an aim never be defined in terms of activity or methods. It must always relate directly to how life is better for everyone. The aim of the system must be clear to everyone in the system. The aim must include plans for the future. The aim is a value judgment.

W. Edwards Deming, American statistician (1900 - 1993)

In January 2012, a group of 21 thought leaders, idea farmers, management coaches, consultants, and practitioners got together in Stoos, Switzerland (FIGURE 2), with the goal to "discuss how to accelerate change in management and organizational transformation". The event was organized by Steve Denning, Franz Röösli, Peter Stevens, and yours truly. It was the most exhausting and rewarding learning experience I had in a long time.

Aside from enthusiastic support and encouraging messages, the Stoos participants also experienced a bit of a backlash, both during and after the Stoos Gathering. We were accused by some of "not being open and transparent".

What did we do wrong?

Well, to be honest, the organizers (including me) were guilty of announcing *publicly* that we were organizing a *private* event, and we asked our readers and followers for input. Such public announcements (and requests for input) had not happened with earlier private events, such as the ones that led to the *Agile Manifesto*[6] and the *Declaration of Interdependence*[7]. Unfortunately, our openness *before* the event conflicted with some of the invitees' need for privacy *during* the event. As a group we decided to respect this need for privacy, which led to our (relative)

[6] Agile Manifesto, http://agilemanifesto.org/

[7] Declaration of Interdependence, http://pmdoi.org/

silence on the social networks while we were talking privately. However, while earlier events before didn't broadcast anything to the outside world while they were still going on, some people found our sudden silence unsettling. And they voiced this concern openly and loudly. None of the organizers had anticipated this.

FIGURE 2: View on Stoos, from the hotel

In hindsight, the feedback was understandable and obvious. In complexity thinking we call it *retrospective coherence*. We had not predicted it, but after the facts it was perfectly comprehensible. Unfortunately, without direct experience organizing such an event, it is impossible to manage these unknowns. We can only learn and iterate, inspect and adapt.

As a change agent it is important to value all discussions, the good ones *and* the bad ones. Because, when people criticize what you're doing, it means they care about the topic. It would have been worrying if the silence among our readers and followers had been more deafening than our own during the event. Furthermore, as someone pointed out, the heated debates were a reflection of the complexity of the problem we were trying to address. If everyone simply agreed, there wouldn't be a problem in the first place!

In this chapter, we will dive deeper into this topic of continuous improvement, or continuous change management.

Inspect and Adapt (and Anticipate and Explore)

An organization is a complex adaptive system (FIGURE 3). It will adapt to what you do, so you must adapt continuously to how the system responds. This is reflected in the words *inspect* and *adapt*, used frequently in the Agile community.

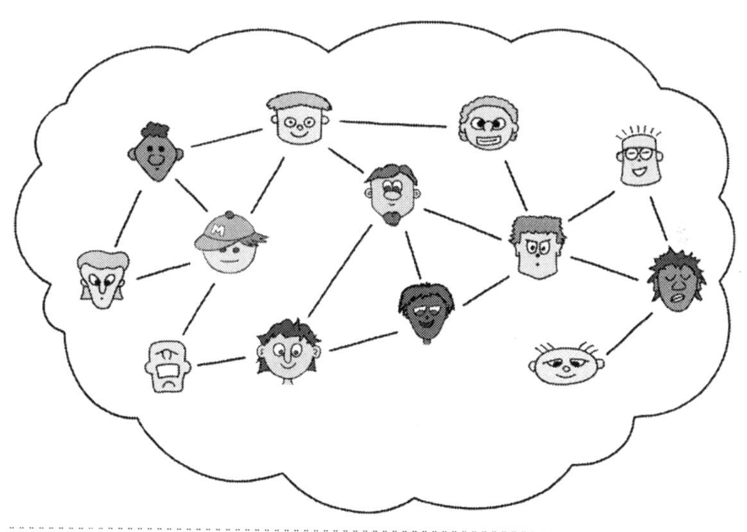

FIGURE 3: An organization as a complex adaptive system

But... adaptation is not enough. If adaptation is all you do, it means the system is always in the lead. People who never steer a system are merely following where it's going! And thus, as a change agent, you have to augment adaptation with *anticipation* and *exploration*. Or, in other words...

> We can't control systems or figure them out. But we can dance with them!
>
> - Donella Meadows, *Thinking in Systems* [Meadows 2008]

The PDCA Model

This is not new. In fact, some of the earliest system thinkers, W. Edwards Deming and Walter A. Shewhart, already described this principle many decades ago. Their *PDCA* model (FIGURE 4) was developed by Shewhart in the early 1920's and made popular by Deming in the 1950's.

FIGURE 4: **PDCA (Plan, Do, Check, Act)**

PDCA, which stands for *Plan*, *Do*, *Check*, *Act*, is an iterative four-step improvement process. Each of your change management initiatives consists of a sequence of interventions in a system (or its environment), where you check the effects the interventions have on the system (or on you). When your actions work as intended, you move on to the next step. When they don't work, you try something else. It is a never-ending cycle of *setting goals* (Plan), *implementing ideas* (Do), *measuring feedback* (Check) and *analyzing results* (Act).

Dancing with a system is about leading and following. It is an ongoing cycle of planning a direction, making a step, sensing the response, and evaluating success. It combines anticipation, adaptation, and exploration.

The concept of PDCA is based on the scientific method of *hypothesis*, *experimentation*, and *evaluation*. There are many alternative models available, such as *Assess-Analyze-Metricate-Improve* [Pulford 1996], *Define-Measure-Improve-Control-Analyze*[8], and *Build-Measure-Learn* [Ries 2011],

---

[8] Six Sigma, http://en.wikipedia.org/wiki/Six_Sigma

but I prefer to stick with the good old *Plan-Do-Check-Act* model, because it is simple, yet effective enough for my purpose.

Especially in the case of inexperienced dancers, the inevitable intermediate results of going in a wrong direction, stepping on someone's toes, or colliding with other initiatives, is for many people the most challenging aspect of change management. There's just one remedy: Learn to be a better dancer.

Plan

I don't believe that people don't like change. The internet, the iPad, and Lady GaGa have proven the opposite. However, I am willing to believe that people don't like *your* suggestion for change. I am quite sure they will actively resist your change because they are not convinced they should change *with* you. Let's see how we can fix that problem.

What Is Your Goal?

First of all, to get people moving, they need a *goal.* They need something to change for. It is vital to make it clear what you want to achieve. Can you paint a picture of a better world? Or a better organization? Can you describe a vision and destination that people will want to believe in? And are you able to use stories, metaphors, and visuals to better get your message across?

> When there is a genuine vision (as opposed to the all-too familiar "vision statement"), people excel and learn, not because they are told to, but because they want to.
>
> - Peter M. Senge, *The Fifth Discipline* [Senge 2006]

- In February 2011 I wanted Agile and Lean practitioners in Europe to collaborate better across borders, because I noticed little interaction between communities in different countries. I crafted a vision of European communities working together. In several blog posts I pointed out what we could achieve by painting a picture of a better world [Appelo 2011e]. It worked! A few months later 40 people from all over Europe got together and turned their hopes and dreams for Agile Lean Europe into a physical Lego model (FIGURE 5), with an explanation on YouTube[9]. This physical visualization helped to make the shared vision even more tangible and concrete.

FIGURE 5: Agile Lean Europe vision[10]

Where Is It Going Well?

Once you know the destination, the best way to get started is to find an example of things going well somewhere, and then to copy the good behaviors. Try to find a situation that can act as a shining example of how you want things to be, or in other words, find a bright spot of good behavior.

In many change initiatives you don't have to start from scratch. You just look for things that are already working well, and start with those. Don't focus too much on the final outcome, focus on the initial behaviors. And not on all of them, but on a few vital ones that can make all the difference.

- Peter Stevens, a Scrum coach, told me that, whenever he starts coaching a new team, he asks people the question, "What was your best project?" He says that, when people share their best practices in a story-telling mode, they always can identify common sense practices that other people would call Agile or Lean. But, he says, "I don't tell the teams to do

[9] ALE network vision, http://www.youtube.com/watch?v=Zg2PMv8lFUA

[10] Picture by Olaf Lewitz, Agile42, used with permission

Scrum or Kanban. If their current project is not their best project, I ask them what it would be like if this project became their best? This helps them to apply practices and approaches that they have just rediscovered."

Your request for change might be hard for many people. Don't make it any harder by requiring big steps in unknown territory. Show them that where you want to go is actually a nice place to be, and then agree on the first simple steps.

Do

You cannot introduce change if you don't know what you want people to do. How would you *define* "good behavior"? What are the few critical moves that people should make?

What Are the Crucial Steps?

To get people going, start with small steps. Don't just throw the big picture at them, but also give them clear and achievable short-term goals. Yes, a grand vision is necessary. But the crucial steps to go in that direction should be simple enough for everyone to understand.

- In 2001, at the Snowbird ski resort in Utah, 17 people got together to discuss better ways of creating software. They came up with a vision that was grand and compelling (FIGURE 6). And they made it concrete by giving it the name "Agile" and turned it into a manifesto[11]. But, individually, these people spent much more time teaching people simple crucial practices, like "write stories on sticky notes" and "show your work on a whiteboard" and "get feedback from your customer every week".

Successful change initiatives often combine a grand vision with simple yet crucial practices.

---

[11] Agile Manifesto, http://agilemanifesto.org/

MANIFESTO FOR AGILE SOFTWARE DEVELOPMENT

WE ARE UNCOVERING BETTER WAYS OF DEVELOPING SOFTWARE BY DOING IT AND HELPING OTHERS DO IT. THROUGH THIS WORK WE HAVE COME TO VALUE:

INDIVIDUALS AND INTERACTIONS OVER PROCESSES AND TOOLS
WORKING SOFTWARE OVER COMPREHENSIVE DOCUMENTATION
CUSTOMER COLLABORATION OVER CONTRACT NEGOTIATION
RESPONDING TO CHANGE OVER FOLLOWING A PLAN

THAT IS, WHILE THERE IS VALUE IN THE ITEMS ON THE RIGHT, WE VALUE THE ITEMS ON THE LEFT MORE.

KENT BECK
MIKE BEEDLE
ARIE VAN BENNEKUM
ALISTAIR COCKBURN
WARD CUNNINGHAM
MARTIN FOWLER
JAMES GRENNING
JIM HIGHSMITH
ANDREW HUNT
RON JEFFRIES
JON KERN
BRIAN MARICK
ROBERT C. MARTIN
STEVE MELLOR
KEN SCHWABER
JEFF SUTHERLAND
DAVE THOMAS

FIGURE 6: The Manifesto for Agile Software Development

When and Where Do You Start?

Timing and location can be very important for some change initiatives. You want to carefully pick the right time and the right place to get started. Sometimes this means you should wait a while for a more appropriate situation. Other times it means you should not wait any longer, and do it now! For example, tickling a system the right way can have a wonderful effect when the system is relaxed and sensitive, but maybe not when the system is giving a keynote speech in front of a large and critical audience.

- For two years I had ideas about a pan-European collaboration of Agile and Lean practitioners. But only after my book was released, and I realized I had people's attention, and I was connecting with people all over Europe, I suddenly understood that the momentum was right there. I had to stop thinking about it and do it!

Doing change management includes figuring out the crucial steps for people to take, and choosing the right time and place to get started.

Check

The third part of the PDCA cycle is about feedback. When you poke the system with ideas you have to check and understand how the system responds.

How Do You Get Feedback?

As a change agent you will try many different things. You have to validate what works and get rid of what doesn't. In other words, you need feedback. But who will be positively critical, and is able to give you feedback you can actually use? You must find people whose opinions are valuable. Get them to munch over your ideas and listen to what they have to say. Experiment with subjects who are willing to suffer the consequences of your ideas and who are glad to report their findings, preferably without punching you in the face.

- When I started giving my Management 3.0 course I experimented several times with different audiences. The first time was a 5-hour workshop at the Scrum Gathering in Amsterdam. The second time was a free 1-day course with 15 people. The third time was a full 2-day beta-test with 30 employees of a paying customer. And even after dozens of courses I still haven't finished experimenting and validating. I usually invite students to post comments on a *happiness door* [Appelo 2011d] just before lunch (FIGURE 7). Such qualitative feedback helps me to improve the course, and keep steering it in the right direction.

FIGURE 7: Feedback during a course

How Do You Measure Results?

Comments are great but qualitative feedback is often not enough. If you don't measure quantitative results, you may not know whether your change initiative is on track. How does that work? How can you measure something as abstract as "becoming Agile" or "being a learning organization"? I'm glad I don't have to answer that question, because this depends on your desired change, and it is something you will need to figure out for yourself. At the same time you must prevent your metrics from leading to dysfunctional system behaviors. Does that sound difficult? Good, because it is!

- Schiphol Airport measures how many people per flight buy tax-free products, where travelers are coming from, and where they are going to. I measure how many students are willing to give me evaluations, which parts of the course they like best, and how they rate the entire course.

Change agents measure things so that they can correlate outcomes with ideas. What did we do that caused a significant change? Was the outcome good? If not, can we try something else? In *The Lean Startup* Eric Ries calls it "validated learning" [Ries 2011]. It is all about measuring which interventions actually have the right effect on people (and which ones don't).

Act

Short feedback cycles are better than long ones. Knowing whether or not something works, prevents you from investing for too long in a bad approach.

How Do You Accelerate Results?

Fast feedback reduces the risk of getting it wrong, and gives you more leeway to experiment. And when things are still fresh in people's minds there are more details that they can reflect upon when they give you feedback.

- One reason I ask students to write comments several times during a course is to capture feedback before they forget it. At first I didn't even read the comments until I got home. (What if they didn't like what I was doing? The horror!) But soon I started reading them during the breaks, so I could act immediately whenever possible. I could respond to feedback after lunch and collect new feedback about the changes only a few hours later!

But perhaps the most important aspect of fast feedback is its potential for triggering a *reinforcing* feedback loop. Short feedback cycles enable you to use quick wins as evidence that your change is worth the effort. Once you have validated that your idea has beneficial outcomes, you can gradually speed up your change and spread it throughout the organization. Quick wins can trigger an amplifying feedback loop that helps you to consolidate gains and produce even more positive change.

Arne Åhlander, consultant in Lund, Sweden

I remember a discussion from a few years ago about which requirements to choose in a project. Some were really big and important and some were small and important. Which ones should we choose? In order for us to understand priorities we pictured two roads merging into one. From one road there came buses (big requirements) and from the other one bicycles (small requirements). At first glance we thought we should let buses go first. On second thought, we believed that in some instances it would be better to let some bicycles through. To me it is like choosing between Kaizen (continuous change in small steps) and Kaikaku (radical change in bigger steps). It is good to have some sort of heuristic for guiding your choice.

Be a Complexity Thinker

A social system is complex and adaptive. As a change agent you have to keep poking it with ideas and check how it responds and changes. And you have to respond to those changes as if you're dancing with the system, carefully guiding it in the right direction.

This means, if you're serious about change, you have to ask yourself some serious questions…

- What Is My Goal?
- Where Is It Going Well?
- What Are the Crucial Steps?
- When and Where Do I Start?
- How Do I Get Feedback?
- How Do I Measure Results?
- How Do I Accelerate Results?

Mind the People

Most people are other people.
Their thoughts are someone else's opinions,
their lives a mimicry,
their passions a quotation.

Oscar Wilde, Irish writer (1854 - 1900)

Our goal for the Stoos Gathering was to achieve an understanding of the problem with managed organizations around the world, an agreement on the desired future, and at least some suggestions for how to get there faster.

The participants defined the problem in the form of "a fifty-dimensional mind-map"[12], as Steve Denning called it. It was rather comprehensive in terms of root causes and consequences. But it was intentionally called a "work in progress". Not in the least because, as we've seen in the last chapter, the problems themselves are always evolving.

The group defined an idealized future as follows:

> "
> Organizations can become learning networks of individuals creating value, and the role of leaders should include the stewardship of the living rather than the management of the machine.

Some would say this grand goal is not measurable, and they would be right. But the 21 participants found the communiqué that emerged at the

[12] Stoos problem definition, http://www.stoosnetwork.org/what-is-the-problem/

end properly reflected their hopes and dreams, and they hoped others would find it inspiring too.

Of course, as change agents, we know that real progress is made with small measurable steps. And in order to do that, the group at Stoos also discussed stakeholders, influencers, and strategies. And we addressed the need to answer the questions, "What's in it for me?" and "How can I do this?" Change will not happen when people see it as something that doesn't benefit them personally, or something that they're unable to implement. That's why, in this chapter, we will discuss how to enable change for people at the *individual* level.

Lift the Barriers

The crucial parts of a social system are the individuals in it (FIGURE 8). And since all people are different, there's no one-approach-fits-all for social change. If you need an organization to improve, you have to work with people's individual needs, and the various barriers people put up in their minds.

FIGURE 8: Individuals in a social network

"

> Designers will find that most organizations can be considerably improved just within the context of the bounded design. This is because the barriers to change are usually in the decision-makers' own minds and in the organization itself.
>
> - Michael C. Jackson, *Systems Thinking* [Jackson 2003]

If you want to change an organization at the level of the individuals, you could hire a neurosurgeon. But it's cheaper, and more effective, to apply the ADKAR model, created by Jeff Hiatt [Hiatt 2006].

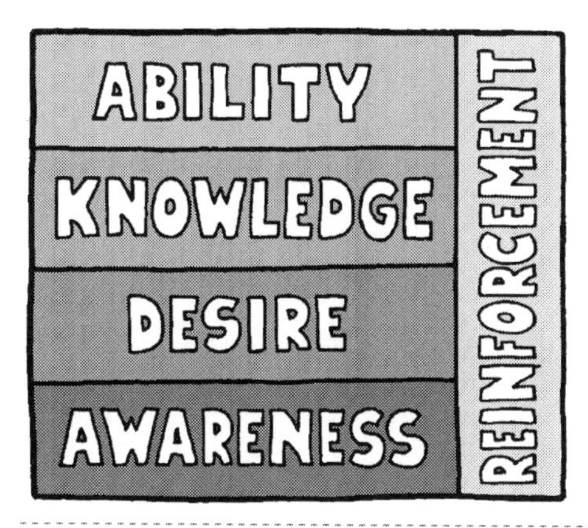

FIGURE 9: ADKAR (Awareness, Desire, Knowledge, Ability, Reinforcement)

The ADKAR Model

ADKAR (FIGURE 9) is a goal-oriented change management model, developed to guide activities during the change process. The model can be used to make sure you don't forget the people aspect in your change initiative.

The ADKAR model has the following five dimensions:

- **Awareness** of the need to change
- **Desire** to participate in and give support for the change
- **Knowledge** of how to change (and what change looks like)
- **Ability** to implement the change on a day-to-day basis
- **Reinforcement** to keep the change in place

What makes the ADKAR model so useful is that it reminds you that a successful personal change of the people in an organization usually requires your attention in multiple areas.

- It's not enough for people to be *aware* of the need for change. They also must *desire* the change.
- Desire is insufficient when people have no *knowledge* of how to change, or when they don't have the *ability* to change.
- And even if they know how, and are able to change, without any *reinforcement* of good behaviors, people will just fall back into old habits.

When you start a change initiative, you may want to consider using the ADKAR model to address change at the individual level in all five dimensions, and lift the barriers in people's heads. I will describe the model in the remainder of this chapter.

Awareness

To move people forward in your change program, a simple notification that tells them to "do things differently, starting next Monday" is usually insufficient, no matter how urgent *you* think the change is.

How Will You Communicate?

Most people are not so good at communicating their ideas. Barack Obama did not become president of the United States while mumbling inaudibly, using incomprehensible words, looking at the ground, and killing his audience with eight dozen bullet points. Nor did his supporters use posters with tiny letters, in bad handwriting, with fading ink, on brown paper bags. Amazingly, I've seen change agents try to deliver their messages in exactly the way I have just described.

You will have to repeat your message constantly, and in many different ways. I have learned that a small investment in communication skills can pay off nicely. For example, the book *Made to Stick* teaches you to deliver your message with simple, unexpected, concrete, credible, emotional stories [Heath 2007].

- Every cigarette package in my country screams "smoking kills", but on most people it has no effect (FIGURE 10). That's because communication is only the first step toward change. It's insufficient, but it's a start. You must learn to touch people's minds with deliberate care and precision, and you should have good stories and pictures to back up your ideas.

FIGURE 10: Did this convince you to stop smoking?[13]

> "
>
> When a smoker is told to stop smoking, the typical response is to continue or increase the rate.
>
> - W. Warner Burke, *Organization Change: Theory and Practice* [Burke 2010]

---

[13] © Shahbaz Majeed, "Smoking Kills", Creative Commons Attribution 2.0 Generic (CC BY 2.0), http://www.flickr.com/photos/ajnabee/18211729/

How Will You Set an Example?

Seeing is believing. There's no greater motivator than a leader who is leading by example. For many people what you actually *do* is far more important than what you *say*. Therefore, you should not only make people aware by *telling* them what you want. You should also be *showing* them how your vision is implemented by practicing what you preach.

- I was better able to help my organization become more Agile by adopting Agile practices in my own daily work. Other people more easily became aware of the need for change when they saw what I was doing.

Making people aware of the need for change involves good communication, which is something you can learn, and setting the right example so others can follow.

Desire

Creating awareness is the first step toward change. But as a change agent you must understand that it's never enough to make people only aware of your idea. Your *rational* messages need to be complemented with *emotional* triggers for change.

How Do You Make It Urgent?

Many times people ignore what is *important* and instead they focus on what is *urgent* [Covey 2004]. Unfortunately, many problems don't manifest themselves in urgent ways. And thus, little happens. People might recognize the importance of your idea, but they don't feel the urgency of it. Therefore, in order to get people to change, you must try and make them *feel* the crisis, and let them experience your idea as something that is also urgent and not just important.

- My father knew it was important to eat healthier food, but for him it was never urgent. Until the time he went to see the doctor because he wasn't feeling very well. The doctor diagnosed severe cardiovascular problems, and gave my father only a few months to live, unless he immediately and radically changed his diet. Now *that* felt urgent! And so he changed.

How Do You Make It Desirable?

People not only change when they feel the urgency of your idea. They also change their behaviors when it makes them feel better! Therefore, if you want people to change, you should try to address their intrinsic desires (FIGURE 11). Target their needs for *status*, *order*, *honor*, *purpose*, or *curiosity*. Tap into their desire to feel *competent*, *independent*, *accepted*, *powerful*, and *socially related*.[14] Mothers know they can feed their children medicines with spoons full of honey. Change agents know they might have to feed people good ideas with spoons full of irresistible effects. (And for some people it is the status quo that is most desirable. In such cases you will have to be creative!)

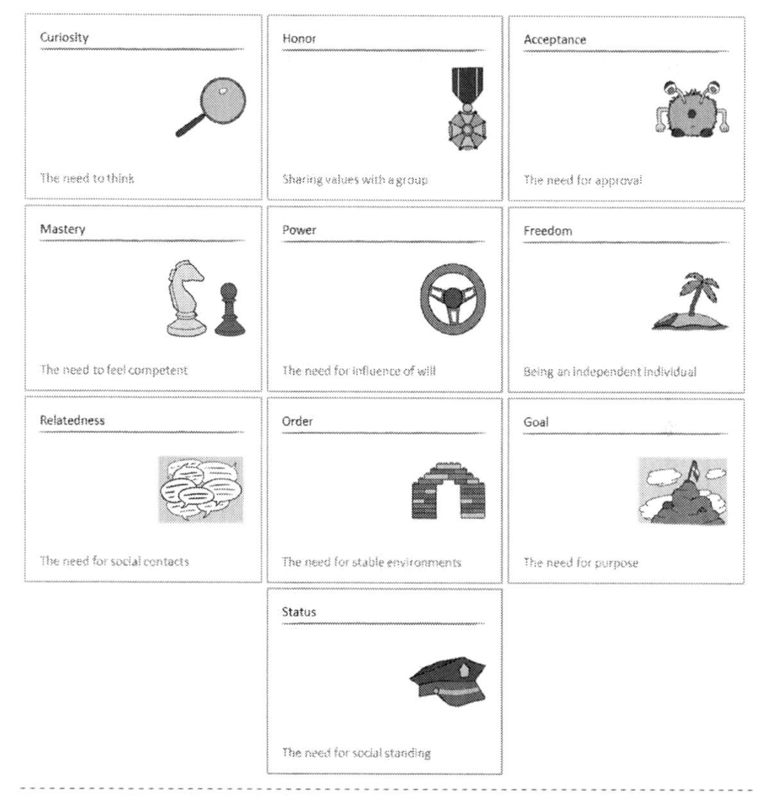

FIGURE 11: The 10 intrinsic desires (with mnemonic "champfrogs")

---

[14] The ten intrinsic desires as described in [Appelo 2011a], page 136

- When I introduced Scrum in the organization where I worked not long ago, nearly everyone liked it. The development teams liked the change because Scrum introduced *order* in our chaotic environment. Management liked it because of the *status* it gave them as leaders of a modern and trendy company. And customers liked it because it gave them more *power* over the backlog and its many weekly changes.

Note that the desirable effects of your ideas don't have to be rational. If people like your idea better when it's blue, big, and fluffy, you know you will have to paint it head-to-toe, pad it in foam, and coat it in feathers.

> "
>
> As it turns out, it's the desire to be accepted, respected, and connected that really pulls at human heart strings. And as far of the rest of us are concerned—managers, parents, and coaches—learn how to co-opt this awesome power, and you can change just about anything.
>
> - Kerry Patterson, *Influencer* [Patterson 2008]

For some people a change is undesirable because they fear some perceived effects of the change. As a change agent you must figure out how a change is affecting people's intrinsic desires. Maybe there is something you can do to alleviate the fears.

- One software developer resisted the introduction of Scrum because it required him to share his code with other developers. He didn't like that because his code was of higher quality and he didn't want others to make a mess of his work. I figured out that competence and status were important for this guy, and so I offered him an informal position as coordinator of quality practices across multiple Scrum teams. He eagerly embraced the idea and from that moment he was a strong supporter of Scrum.

When you want people to change it is not enough to simply send them an email with a rational explanation for the change. You have to make them feel the change is both urgent *and* desirable.

Knowledge

So, the people are aware of the need for change, and they have a desire to do something about it. What then? Will they immediately understand what to do? Will they implement change exactly as you had intended?

Who Will Be Teaching?

Some people need help adopting a change, and it is important to consider who will assist them. A recognized expert can sometimes make more of a difference than a smart colleague, even when they both say exactly the same thing. Mentors, coaches, and gurus may assist you in guiding people in their journey toward change. Whether it is via courses, consultancy, books, or webinars, the voice of the expert can be a significant help in your endeavor.

- A student in my course recently told me how much the training had inspired her to change as a manager. She confessed that my course didn't actually contain any new information for her. She knew most of it already, she said. (I tried to smile understandingly at this point.) But the fact that I was there to explain it all again, made all the difference. (At this point my smile became more sincere.)

How Will You Teach Them?

The way a trainer teaches something is as important as the message itself. Since lectures seldom inspire people, it is better to communicate an idea using stories, exercises, games, and discussions. Try to make people laugh. Or cry. Move their minds and their bodies. And allow them to teach each other.

- When I prepared the development of my Management 3.0 course I researched popular brain science literature, such as *Brain Rules* [Medina 2008] and *Enriching the Brain* [Jensen 2006], and books for teachers and trainers, such as *Training from the Back of the Room* [Bowman 2009] and *Thiagi's 100 Favorite Games* [Thiagarajan 2006]. These books told me that lectures are the *least* effective technique for trainers. People learn best when they interact with each other and with their environment, using multiple senses and multiple techniques. That's why I prefer to have people play games and share conversations. (Of course, I do give small lectures for about 20 minutes per topic. How else would I justify my fee?)

People need to know what to do in order to implement change successfully. You can help them by inviting experts to assist people in their change, and by applying interactive learning techniques.

Ability

For many people change is a difficult and overwhelming experience. It looks like everything has to be done *differently* and *right now*, but the situation they find themselves in simply doesn't allow them to do what is expected of them.

What Makes It Easy?

As a change agent you should help to remove any obstacles that prevent people from adopting the desired behaviors. Even with awareness, desire, and knowledge properly in place, a small step can still be extremely hard to make when a person's situation is working against it.

- At the ALE 2011 unconference we did our best to involve people from all European countries. We selected Berlin because it's roughly in the middle of Europe (which made traveling easier); we initially kept places available for small countries (by setting a maximum number of participants per country); and we even tried to help speakers from countries with low wages (assisting them with low-cost travel and accommodation). We did all that to make pan-European collaboration easier for everyone. (It worked so well that there were 34 European countries represented, "including" Canada and the US.)

How Can They Practice?

For many people, change takes skill and practice. Even if they want to change, they often cannot do this overnight. It requires time and effort to learn how to do things well. Give people the space and the means to learn, and to practice their skill and discipline in order to do a good job.

- Professional software developers learn how to be great programmers with practices such as code retreats and coding dojos. But this requires them to remove barriers, taking some time off from work and busy projects every now and then, to spend time honing their skills. Software developers are like musicians and athletes who can only perform well with a good amount of practice.

Even when people are willing to change, their situation is sometimes holding them back. Change agents work on removing barriers and making room for practice.

Reinforcement

I'm sure you recognize this. Early January you decide that *this* year will be the year you will *finally* start working out/stop watching TV/become a vegetarian/call your parents/___ (fill-in-the-space). But, despite some promising initial activities, in February you find yourself, again, on the couch, with a hamburger, watching a program about dysfunctional families. People often show some good efforts to change, but then they fall back into old patterns and familiar habits.

What Are the Short-Term Wins?

When people change, they need to see and feel they're doing a good job. The higher goal is often a destination far ahead on the road. Make sure you celebrate small successes, so people know they're heading in the right direction and want to continue working to achieve the next small success. Provide evidence that they're making progress and that this is worth their ongoing commitment.

- Several times in my life I started writing a book. And several times I failed. I simply lost the will to keep going. But then I decided to write a blog (FIGURE 12). And after a few blog posts I received some comments, and compliments. It turned out that this feedback from readers was exactly what I needed to write another blog post. And another. And before I knew it I had written enough materials to show to a publisher and turn it into a book. My long-term goal (write a book) had slowly but steadily become achievable while I was celebrating many short-term wins.

FIGURE 12: Why I started my blog

What Makes It Sustainable?

The sustainability of new behavior is best achieved when you can turn the boring parts of it into something that is fun. Consider anchoring your new approach in people's minds by adding social, competitive, or other addictive dimensions, so that people want to keep on doing it. Sometimes you have to come up with something complicated to reinforce the good behavior; but quite often a mere "thank you" is enough to acknowledge that people did a good job, and keep them going.

- In the new smartphone era, some people keep track of their physical exercises online, and they compete with friends on social networks. This makes the good behavior (working out) sustainable by adding a social and addictive aspect (gaming), which leads to reinforcement of the desired behavior.

Both the focus on short-term wins and the addition of a social dimension can help you tremendously to achieve behaviors that are sustainable over time.

Be a People Person

When you want people to change, sending rational messages to them is usually not enough. Treat people as emotional beings who can use a little help on the way, in communication and collaboration with others.

This means that, if you're serious about change, you have to ask yourself some serious questions…

- How Will I Communicate?
- How Will I Set an Example?
- How Do I Make It Urgent?
- How Do I Make It Desirable?
- Who Will Be Teaching?
- How Will I Teach Them?
- What Makes It Easy?
- How Can They Practice?
- What Are the Short-Term Wins?
- What Makes It Sustainable?

Stimulate the Network

Men cling passionately to old traditions and display intense reluctance to modify customary modes of behavior, as innovators at all times have found to their cost. The dead-weight of conservatism, largely a lazy and cowardly distaste for the strenuous and painful activity of real thinking, has undoubtedly retarded human progress...

V. Gordon Childe, Australian archaeologist (1892 - 1957)

The 21 people who convened at Stoos in Switzerland delivered an outcome that was, in the eyes of some, not world-shaking. This complaint was voiced several times, even before the event was finished, and before participants had a chance to sleep, travel, and prepare and publish blog posts or produce videos. At the same time, other people were inspired by our little event and initiated spin-off events on their own.

Of course, both our critics and our followers were right. The Stoos event was meant to make a first step, to form a "guiding coalition", and to discuss *how* to make the next steps. It was not intended to solve the world's biggest problems in only 1.5 days. But the feedback we received confirmed a vital point about change management. Most change initiatives start with a small group of supporters, a small group of skeptics, and a big group of people who don't care. When you hear both positive and negative feedback about the things you're doing, there is no reason to get confused. On the contrary, now is the time to prepare yourself for the path that will take you along the curve of yay-sayers, nay-sayers, and get-out-of-my-way-sayers.

Follow the Curve

An organization is a network and, as in every social complex system, behaviors spread through an organization like viruses (FIGURE 13). As the Agile Manifesto says, it's about *individuals* and their *interactions*. If you want to be a change agent in your organization, awareness of the network can help you to overcome resistance to change, and transform an entire social system.

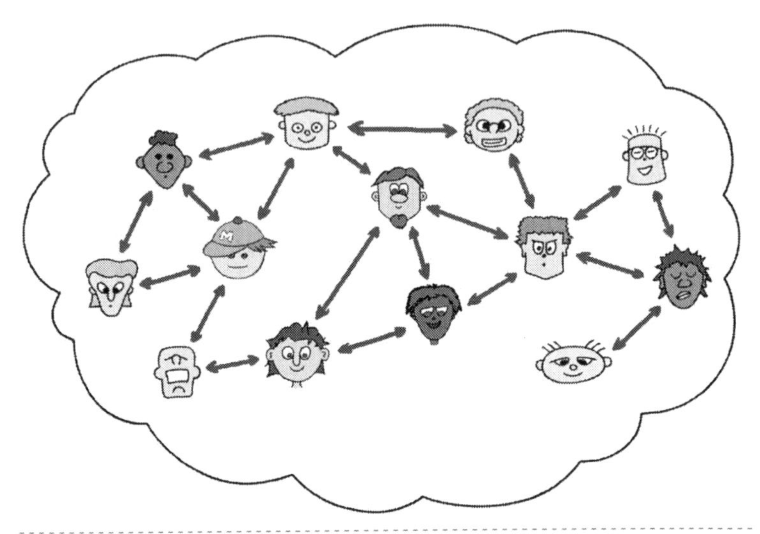

FIGURE 13: An organization as a social network

The Adoption Curve

The rate of adoption of behavior is the relative speed with which a change or innovation is adopted. A crucial point is the moment when a behavior reaches *critical mass*, or a tipping point [Gladwell 2000]. That's the point within the adoption curve where so many individuals participate, that further adoption can become self-reinforcing.

But how do you achieve that critical mass?

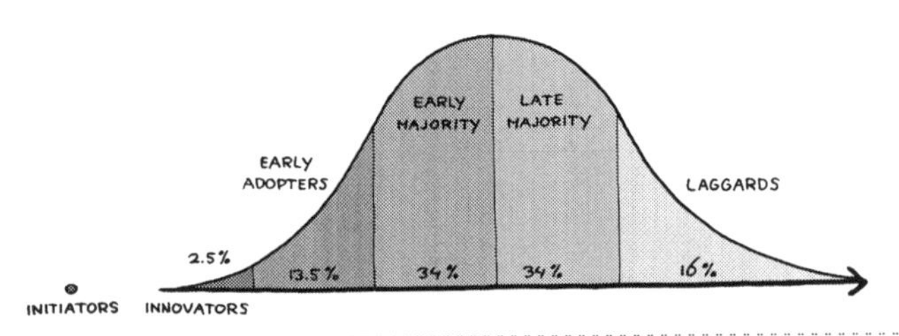

FIGURE 14: The Innovation Adoption curve

Professor Everett Rogers produced a theory in 1962, called the *Diffusion of Innovations* [Rogers 2003], in which he explained that *innovators* are the first to support a new idea in a social network. They are followed by *early adopters*, an *early* and *late majority*, and a group of *laggards* (FIGURE 14). For change agents like you and me, the trick is to reach out to these different kinds of people in the network with different approaches and different messages.

- Note: I added an extra category called *initiators* to Rogers' model. The initiators (some people call them "igniters") are the change agents themselves, the ones who desire a change of behavior in other people.

The adoption curve is not a party tent. There is no one-size-fits-all. When you are leading a change in your organization, you will work with different messages and methods in order to address different people. What works for the innovators will probably not work with the majority. And the way you convince the early adopters will certainly not be successful with the laggards.

In this chapter we will review the different groups in the network, and how to use this categorization to your advantage.

Initiators

The group of change agents is the first one we should discuss. That's you! Many people would love to be an initiator or igniter of a change program, but they don't create the right conditions for themselves to do a good job.

Are You Committed?

No change effort can succeed without change agents being fully committed. Can you set aside the time and energy that is needed to actually pull it off? Are you dedicated to your cause and your goal, and not distracted all the time by other work and projects?

- At ISM eCompany, as the Chief Information Officer, I was very committed when I introduced Scrum in the organization. Continuous improvement was an essential part of my job, and

I could spend as much time as I thought was needed. I won't claim I did a spectacularly good job, but that was not for lack of available resources. Sure, I realize that many people don't find themselves in such a luxurious position. But they *will* have to find other ways to create the right conditions.

Who Is Assisting You?

Successful change agents rarely work alone. Try to involve some friends or colleagues you can trust to help you win over the rest of the organization. Many initiators create a "guiding coalition" of people who help them, either openly or behind the scenes [Kotter 1996]. You must find people who care about you and the change program you're working on. Have the guts to involve others, especially when they have more knowledge and experience in the social network than you have.

- When I started working on the Agile Lean Europe network, I asked several good contacts to help me grow the pan-European community. Via e-mail and a private forum, we discussed our approach and we monitored how the environment responded to our messages.

Ensuring the right amount of time, energy, and friends is a precondition for all successful change agents. Even President Obama, a Nobel Prize-winning change agent, isn't working by himself. He has succeeded where others have failed (granted, not in *all* areas, but at least in *some*) because he surrounds himself with advisors and helpers, and he spent an amazing amount of time and energy to make things happen.

Yves Ferland, Agile coach in Montréal, Canada

I think the coaching part is most of the time ignored or poorly executed. I found that providing individual coaching, especially to the innovators and early adopters, maximizes the chances at building the critical amount of promoters inside the organization. People willing to make changes, need first and foremost to work on themselves. Like in aircraft safety procedures, parents are told to put on the oxygen mask first prior to helping their kids. Likewise, people making plans for changes and following good practices, will only be as good as their capabilities at sensing their environment. If the change agents are no good at correctly reading the emotional states of the people going through a change, they will act incorrectly and will only make a mess of things.

Innovators

Every change program starts with a first selection of people who are most likely to convert and adopt the change.

Who Will Be the Innovators?

Look for the innovators in your organization and figure out what motivates them. Find out where in the social network it is best to start the change and win the innovators over by offering them something they cannot possibly resist, because they see the change as specifically designed for *them.*

- Innovators are the ones who were standing in lines for hours when the iPad was launched. They were the people who attended the official launch of my book when it was just released. And they were the readers who first commented on my blog when I just got started. It is not uncommon for innovators to receive special treatment from change agents. After all, these are the ones who are supposed to set the whole wave of change in motion.

Change management experts all agree that, certainly in this earliest stage of your change initiative, you should not spend too much time fighting critics and skeptics. Try focusing first on the ones who are most eager and willing to adopt the change, and grow your change program from there. But a word of warning is important here. *Don't* sell your idea to innovators who are not respected by the rest of the people you want to convince. If you sell to the wrong ones, the rest will resist even harder.

> "
>
> The key to getting the majority of any population to adopt a vital behavior is to find out who these [unwanted] innovators are and avoid them like the plague. If they embrace your new idea, it will surely die.
>
> - Kerry Patterson, *Influencer* [Patterson 2008]

Early Adopters

Once you have convinced the first few people to adopt the change, you must proceed and have a look at the next group in the innovation adoption curve.

Who Are the Early Adopters?

Change spreads more easily through a social network when influential people adopt the new behaviors. You will have to find out who the connectors in your organization are [Gladwell 2000]. They are the ones who know everyone and who can influence a lot of people. Focus on trying to get them to join the change program and spread the word.

- There are some who would claim that, in any change effort, it is wise to focus first on secretaries and office managers, because they are in contact with nearly everyone in an organization. This may be somewhat exaggerated, but there's a grain of truth in it. After all, for similar reasons, virus epidemics have been traced back to people who visit lots of airports. That's where the contaminations are most effective.

> "
>
> The point is not to find the average customer but to find early adopters: the customers who feel the need for the product most acutely. Those customers tend to be more forgiving of mistakes and are especially eager to give feedback.
>
> - Eric Ries, *The Lean Startup* [Ries 2011]

How Will the Leaders Help?

Change spreads more easily when recognized leaders are endorsing the change initiative. Try and find some "big name sponsors", or influential people who believe in your ideas and who can bring your change (more quickly) to other parts of the network. By getting social support from powerful figures, celebrities, top managers, competency leaders, or influential study groups, your initiative will be perceived as more valuable in the eyes of others.

> "
> Many early adopters are what are commonly known as opinion leaders. These important people represent about 13.5 percent of the population. They are smarter than average, and tend to be open to new ideas. But they are different from innovators in one critical respect: They are socially connected and respected. And here's the real influence key. The rest of the population—over 85 percent—will not adopt the new practices until opinion leaders do.
>
> - Kerry Patterson, *Influencer* [Patterson 2008]

- In the ALE network we got early support from a number of well-connected authors and speakers, such as Lisa Crispin, Rachel Davies, and J.B. Rainsberger. This helped significantly to increase exposure of the idea to a bigger part of the network.

After the innovators, the group of early adopters is the next in the adoption curve. The "contamination" of the network with your ideas is most effective when the early adopters group contains connectors and leaders, who are able to influence a lot of people. You should try and find out who they are (FIGURE 15).

FIGURE 15: Find out who the leaders are[15]

Early Majority

And then you have a problem. Because after the initiators and the early adopters the next group is the majority, split into an early and a late majority. Most of these people don't really care about your change program. They have better things to do. The innovators and early adopters are genuinely interested in the problem you're trying to solve. But the majority cares more about Justin Bieber. (Or they *do* care about the problem, but they're just more risk-averse.)

How Do You Reach the Early Majority?

At some point you cannot address people individually anymore. You have to rally the herd in another way. At this point you don't need visionary individuals; you need "ordinary" people to pay attention. Therefore, the way you address the majority will be different from the way you address the earlier groups. Geoffrey Moore explains that there is a "chasm" between the early adopters and the early majority [Moore 2002]. Many innovations and change initiatives get stuck because the new behaviors don't cross the chasm.

- The earliest iPads were bought by innovators and early adopters who loved its design, its multi-touch features, and just the fact that it was a new device made by Apple. But the

15 © Alessandro Bonvini, "Leaders and followers II", Creative Commons Attribution 2.0 Generic (CC BY 2.0), http://www.flickr.com/photos/alebonvini/3084776102/

majority of people don't care about such things. The majority cares more about being able to watch movies on the train.

How Can You Make It Viral?

Part of the challenge of reaching the majority is to delegate your work to other people. You cannot communicate the benefits of change to each and every person, and so other people must do this for you. The change initiative must be contagious. There should be some kind of snowball effect. Yes, the metaphors are endless, just like the number of options you have to implement them.

- The best reason for the success of Hotmail and Gmail is that people (the early adopters) used these free email clients to send messages to their friends (the majority). Microsoft and Google didn't have to do anything, except to make sure they could cope with rapidly growing interest because early customers kept exposing their friends to the benefits of free email.

In order to reach the early majority you must take into account that different groups have different needs. What works for the innovators and early adopters probably won't work for the majority. Also, you have to think about the *viral* aspect of the change program. People must become ambassadors for change within their social circles (FIGURE 16), and sometimes even without realizing it.

FIGURE 16: Anonymous and Occupy, two ideas that went viral[16]

Late Majority

And it gets even harder! Once you're able to make your idea show up on the majority's radar, roughly half of that majority will be positively interested in it. The other half will be negatively interested.

How Will You Deal With Skeptics?

With every change initiative there are skeptics. This is not necessarily a bad thing. Skeptics can keep you and your change initiative sharp. By listening to criticism you can often find ways to improve. And improvement leads to short-term wins that can be used to convince more people, and corner the skeptics.

- After being confronted with some skepticism about a European Agile/Lean movement, I learned how to adjust and improve my communication. I had to deal with some painful comments and rumors about my efforts and motivations. It wasn't fun, but it was useful. By tweaking our message, and persisting in communicating short-term wins, we were able to neutralize the skeptics and convince more people. In hindsight, I think the skeptics helped us do a better job.

[16] © Luciano Castillo, "Anonymous Mask", Creative Commons Attribution 2.0 Generic (CC BY 2.0), http://www.flickr.com/photos/luccast85/6250260580/

Keep in mind that you can learn from skepticism, but the effort to convince the real cynics is often a waste of your time. Use the feedback you receive to learn, not to fight. Focus your energy on the rest of the majority. If you handle the criticism well, the resistance to change among the late majority can dissolve faster than you can say "Charley the change agent charged in and changed chubby Chan."

Laggards

We're almost there! But we cannot tick the *Done* checkbox just yet. A change initiative is like redesigning a garden. After all the heavy digging, lifting and pushing is completed, the maintenance phase begins.

How Will You Prevent a Relapse?

Sometimes change initiatives are called "successful" too early, and then unresolved resistance is able to undo all the work. You must keep in touch with the people in your change program and stay pro-active. Now is the time to keep people enthusiastic and monitor that the change is still working. Keep doing this, again and again, until the new behaviors have finally become part of the organizational culture.

- I once heard someone say, "A coach has to leave as soon as an organization has become Agile." But that might be too early. As long as the new behaviors are not anchored in the organizational culture, the laggards who were against it from the start will do everything they can to pull the organization back into old behavioral patterns.

When things are looking good you might be lulled into complacency, or a false sense of completion. Don't cry victory too soon!

Mischa Ramseyer, Agile coach in Zürich, Switzerland

In one project I had some really strong laggards with big influence in the organization. They made it possible to roll back many of the key points of the transformation that I had achieved. This was a really hard experience for me. Reflecting on what happened, I had to admit I had not really established a connection between me and these guys. Maybe I had not rated them as important in my list of stakeholders. This should be a reminder to every change agent that analyzing the stakeholders in a change initiative is part of "Stimulating the Network".

Spread the Idea

Behaviors are transmitted in a social network from person to person. You have to treat your idea as if it is a beneficial virus, and you want it to be contagious.

Therefore, you should to ask yourself some serious questions…

- Am I Committed?
- Who Is Assisting Me?
- Who Will Be the Innovators?
- Who Are the Early Adopters?
- How Will the Leaders Help?
- How Do I Reach the Early Majority?
- How Can I Make It Viral?
- How Will I Deal With Skeptics?
- How Will I Prevent a Relapse?

Change the Environment

We do not know, in most cases, how far social failure and success are due to heredity, and how far to environment. But environment is the easier of the two to improve.

J.B.S. Haldane, British geneticist (1892 - 1964)

One topic that was discussed at the Stoos Gathering was the name and identity of the movement that we felt ourselves part of. How should we call ourselves, when we feel part of the same group of people who are trying to modernize management around the world? What could be the name of follow-up events, if we organize any? How should we brand our social network groups and Twitter stream?

At the time, the participants could not come to a consensus on a word or name that could properly represent us. None of the words we came up with represented the passion we felt for organizational transformation. And thus we decided to stick with "Stoos" as a placeholder term for a while, and we use "Stoos Network" as the name of the LinkedIn group[17], until somebody comes up with something sexier.

Such discussions matter, because the forming of a shared identity is part of creating an environment in which people are gently (or sometimes not so gently) nudged in the direction of change. Tweaking the environment is the last big topic, and we will focus on it in this chapter.

Self-Organization within Boundaries

In modern organizations we see work being done by self-organizing teams. But self-organization isn't the holy grail of effectiveness. In some

[17] Stoos Network, http://www.linkedin.com/groups/?gid=4243114

situations you have to prevent a *Tragedy of the Commons*[18] situation, whereby people or teams optimize only their own work, not taking into account the "greater good" an organization is trying to achieve.

Fortunately, there is a way to deal with this…

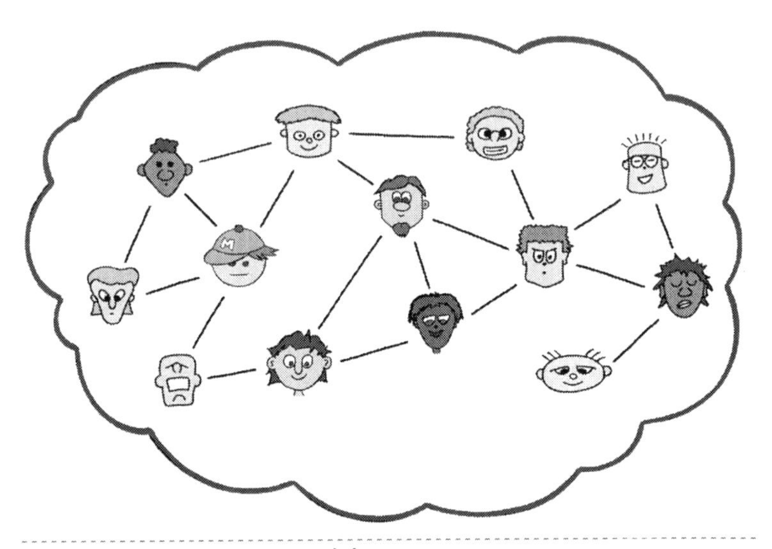

FIGURE 17: The boundary around the system

Self-organization happens within a boundary (FIGURE 17). The environment constrains and influences how people behave. And *you* can tweak the environment. Therefore, when you manipulate the environment, you automatically also manipulate the behavior of people.

The Four I's Plus One

If you want to steer self-organization by changing the environment, you can consider the following suggestions, based on the *Four I's model* proposed by Mark van Vugt [Van Vugt 2009], which I have extended to the *Five I's model* (FIGURE 18):

---

[18] Tragedy of the Commons, http://en.wikipedia.org/wiki/Tragedy_of_the_commons

- *Information*: Use information radiators to make people aware of the consequences of their current behavior.
- *Identity*: Appeal to a higher identity (such as a corporate culture) so that people feel a need to work together.
- *Incentives*: Give small rewards for good behavior, in the form of compliments or tokens of appreciation.
- *Infrastructure*: The tools and infrastructure you set up around people will significantly influence and guide their behaviors.
- *Institutions*: Introduce communities of practice, or other informal institutions, that can set standards for good conduct.

FIGURE 18: The Five I's (Four I's plus one)

Behavior is a function of a person and his or her environment, as was pointed out long ago by psychologist Kurt Lewin with his famous equation:[19]

$B=f(P,E)$

In order to change people's behavior, instead of changing the people themselves (which is hard to do without an expensive operating table), you might want to consider changing the environment, and let the people (re-)organize themselves.

Information

The first suggestion in the Five I's model is usually the easiest to implement. It says that we should make information available to everyone

[19] Wikipedia: Lewin's equation, http://en.wikipedia.org/wiki/Lewin's_equation

about the status of the organization, and about the effects of people's behaviors.

How Do You Radiate Information?

A crucial step in many change programs is to change the environment so that people can better see what is going on. Make sure the progress toward change can be seen by anyone and, even better, show them how their current behavior compares to what is actually needed.

- In traffic management it is well known that dynamic speed displays have a positive effect on the behavior of most drivers [Goetz 2011]. (These are electronic signs, coupled with radar, which tell you how fast you're going, usually in huge digits and an annoyingly big smiley face.) When such a sign says you're going too fast, chances are good you will slow down. Not because you will otherwise be punished (you won't be), but because you didn't realize you were going too fast, or because you don't want to be recognized as a jerk.

> It's amazing how quickly and easily behavior changes can come, with even slight enlargement of bounded rationality, by providing better, more complete, timelier information.
>
> - Donella H. Meadows, *Thinking in Systems* [Meadows 2008]

How Do You Ease Communication?

Sometimes you must help people communicate better so that good behavior spreads more easily across the network. Interaction between people is crucial and should be made as easy as possible. Think about how you can shorten the distance or increase the bandwidth of communication, for instance, by removing walls, replacing stone barriers with glass, handing out Skype headsets, or using social media. Acting like a Dutchman (speaking your mind and being blissfully unaware of other people's sensitivities) can sometimes work wonders too.

- With the conception of the ALE Network I created a LinkedIn group to ease communication among the people who wanted to participate. LinkedIn groups are very accessible, because nearly everyone already has an account. The participants then quickly established the #alenetwork hashtag on Twitter, which enabled them to share ideas more quickly across the network.

Information radiators are all around us. They are in our house, on the streets, and in our work place, and they influence how we are behaving. Wise change agents understand how to use them to their advantage.

Identity

The second part of the Five I's model is more difficult. This one is about the social group as a container that can nudge or pull people to move in the desired direction.

What Is the Group Identity?

In a change process, it often helps to appeal to some identity or brand that people want to associate themselves with. People are social creatures. They like to be part of something larger. And they like to imagine that the coolness of the brand rubs off on them.

- Whenever the Dutch football team (soccer team for Americans) is playing an important international match, Dutch people go around dressed up wearing the most ridiculous clothes with references to Dutch culture (FIGURE 19). And it's all in orange, because that is our national royal color. (I find it interesting that the fans make comments such as "*we* will win the game" and "*we* are the best team", while what really happens is that *we* don't do anything except drink copious amounts of alcohol.)

FIGURE 19: Dutch football fans[20]

How Can You Grow Peer Pressure?

Behavior is contagious when people pressure each other to change. You can tap into the power of peer pressure so that people convince each other to adopt a new behavior, and you don't have to do anything. Peer pressure can do its work for you when people have a strong sense of being part of a social unit, and you are able to connect the desired behavior to the group's identity. Of course, this is every product marketers' dream. And it's not an easy thing to accomplish.

- What the majority of people consider fashionable has often nothing to do with the usefulness of the items themselves, but more with the people wearing them. It is the only explanation for fashion hits such as shoulder pads, small leather ties, and baggy pants. In a similar vein, popular practices among knowledge workers are often applied because they give the workers a sense of belonging, and not so much a sense of effectiveness. It seems to me the only logical explanation for the popularity of business suits, job titles, and meetings.

Don't give your change initiative its own uninteresting and boring name, but instead borrow a brand identity that is already out there and that people feel good about. Try and connect the desired behavior to that

---

[20] © Dan Kamminga, "Orange1", Creative Commons Attribution 2.0 Generic (CC BY 2.0), http://www.flickr.com/photos/dankamminga/174479924/

identity so that peer pressure can work for you and the practice gets popular because it adds to the social cohesion.

Incentives

The third item in the Five I's model is perhaps the most dangerous one. In many organizations managers try to influence people's behaviors with incentives (awards, gifts, bonuses, etc.). Unfortunately, incentives are usually applied badly, and all too often they have nasty side-effects and lead to dysfunctional behaviors [Pink 2009]. However, scientific research says we *can* apply incentives successfully, *if* the desired behaviors are non-creative tasks, and *if* we focus on good behaviors rather than good outcomes, and *if* the rewards are small [Fleming 2011].

Can You Incentivize Good Behavior?

You may want to consider incentives when you need people to perform some uninteresting but nevertheless necessary task. Some examples are cleaning up the kitchen after using it, filling out compliance forms imposed by law, and running security checks after deployment of a software package. Someone has got to do it, so you better make sure they know it is appreciated.

- Incentives are used extensively by animal trainers and parents. Dogs and children get rewards (a compliment, hug, ice cream, or meat cookie) for behaviors that take them in the right direction. And the bar is usually raised higher and higher because the reward should be earned for the *effort* involved. If daily routine has made something easy the reward should not be handed out anymore. Instead, the reward should be reserved for things that still take some effort to do. In the end the meat cookies are only earned when all sheep are herded correctly into the correct field. I can hardly think of a better way to keep your children fit.

Keep in mind that rewarding good *results* differs from rewarding good *behaviors*. Good outcomes (for example, high grades at school) can often be faked, whilst it is usually harder to cheat on good behaviors (for example, doing homework). And the reward should be the smallest possible thing that still works. Quite often a sincere "thank you" or hug is enough. But this depends on the dog.

Infrastructure

I have extended the original Four I's model with *infrastructure* because I believe this option is somewhat different from the others. It also enables me to claim the Five I's model as my own brilliant creation.

Which Barriers Will You Remove?

Change initiatives are often thwarted by barriers in the environment. This prevents people from changing and it inhibits good behaviors from spreading. Therefore, you must ask yourself if you can somehow change the physical or digital infrastructure in which people are working and living, and if you can remove some of the barriers. (Of course, a valid alternative can be *placing* barriers instead of *removing* them.)

- In several areas of my hometown Rotterdam, people were used to taking shortcuts to avoid traffic lights, destroying the neat and tidy green lawns in the process. The government then decided to elevate the curbs so that they are now almost half a meter high. The quality of people's driving skills has increased significantly since then. (And so did the employment in the tire repair business.)

Which Guides Will You Place?

Sometimes all that is needed for people to change is some guidance in the right direction. The behavior of people is not only determined by who they are, but also by the situation they find themselves in. You might be able to change that situation and apply some visual management techniques to influence people's behaviors.

- Schiphol is my favorite airport because it looks good and it's very user friendly (FIGURE 20). The smart design of the signs, screens, escalators, paths, and other visual and physical objects direct me almost automatically to my gate. OK, maybe first to the shops and then to the gates.

FIGURE 20: Schiphol airport[21]

As a change agent you must investigate the environment and decide where you can remove barriers, and where you can provide better guidance. Also note that, sometimes, the barriers are in people's heads, when they simply *believe* they are not able or allowed to do what you desire.

Institutions

Many problems in organizations (or societies) are not caused by a lack of rules, but because of them. And those who know me personally are familiar with my attitude toward rule-crazy governments. However, I admit that sometimes the behavior of people *does* need a bit of governance.

Who Can Make the Rules?

Self-organizing people and teams have a tendency to optimize for themselves. But it is important that people also keep an eye on the organization (or society) as a whole. And it can be useful to introduce some rules, but preferably without a stifling government. The trick is to urge people to come up with some form of governance by themselves.

[21] © Chen Zhao, "Amsterdam Schiphol Airport", Creative Commons Attribution 2.0 Generic (CC BY 2.0), http://www.flickr.com/photos/livepine/269789945/

For instance, you can suggest that they set up communities of practice, which have the power to define organization-wide rules for desired and undesired behaviors.

- After I had introduced Scrum in our organization, the ScrumMasters for various teams regularly got together to discuss rules and procedures. Management was not needed to define these constraints in detail. I merely had to point out some problems, and I nudged people toward possible solutions. And then they were perfectly capable of creating rules with each other.

Governance for good behavior can often be performed by communities of practice or other informal structures.

Try to prevent forming rule-crazy governments for as long as possible. It would make me very happy.

Optimize the Environment

Self-organization always happens within boundaries. If you want people to self-organize in a different direction, then try to optimize the environment instead of the behavior of people. Ask yourself the following questions…

- How Do I Radiate Information?
- How Do I Ease Communication?
- What Is the Group Identity?
- How Can I Grow Peer Pressure?
- Can I Incentivize Good Behavior?
- Which Barriers Will I Remove?
- Which Guides Will I Place?
- Who Can Make the Rules?

Conclusion

Good management is the art of making problems so interesting and their solutions so constructive that everyone wants to get to work and deal with them.

Paul Hawken, American environmentalist (1946)

Sometimes, people literally ask me the question, "How do I change my organization's culture?" My answer is always that you can't directly change the culture of an organization. But if you do what I've described here, and you are successful at changing some behaviors, and the new behaviors are sustainable, then the *emergent outcome* is that you have changed the organization's culture.

> Culture changes only after you have successfully altered people's actions, after the new behavior produces some group benefit for a period of time.
>
> - John P. Kotter, *Leading Change* [Kotter 1996]

With this booklet I hope to have given you some inspiration for changing the world around you. Whether it is a small change initiative, such as trying to convince your team members not to make fun of your Chihuahua, or a big change initiative, such as teaching the whole world to take Chihuahuas more seriously, the Change Management 3.0 model is the same. The questions you should ask yourself apply to almost any kind of change program. Well, at least they applied to each of mine.

- If you need some more guidance on how to answer the change management questions, I suggest you pick up a copy of the book *Fearless Change: Patterns for Introducing New Ideas* [Manns,

Rising 2005]. It contains dozens of patterns you can apply to your own change initiative, in order to increase the chance of success.

Mischa Ramseyer reminded me that only initiators/igniters will be interested in the Change Management 3.0 supermodel. It's intended as a cheat sheet for change agents, not as a guide for the organization. You might want to keep the model in your hand while you do your daily work, but don't bother showing it to the people you want to change. It is unlikely to help.

Changing Management

With initiatives such as *Management 3.0* and the *Stoos Network* I keep trying to convince managers around the world to manage their organizations as *learning networks of diverse individuals creating value.*

Dance with the System

At least, **that is my goal**. With modern organizations such as Whole Foods, W.L. Gore, Semco, Southwest Airlines, Haier, and many others, we already have examples **where this is going well**. And I'm trying to make my own small contribution. The *Management 3.0* course is intended as an indication of the **crucial steps** that managers should take when modernizing their organizations. And I think they should do it *now*. The financial crisis that has hit the US and Europe seems to indicate that right now is a great **time and place to start** with organizational transformations. Fortunately, thanks to social media and intensive traveling, I am guaranteed to get plenty of **feedback** (both anticipated and unanticipated) on my small attempts to change the world. However, although I can measure the number of participants of my courses, and the number of buyers of my book, I am unsure how to actually **measure progress** on a global scale. And **accelerating results** using the feedback I've acquired is also still a work-in-progress.

Mind the People

Over time I have learned **how to communicate** better (which has always been a problem for me). This includes **setting the right example** by managing my own classes, my own business, and various networks of volunteers, in a Management 3.0 kind of way. I probably struggle most with the challenge of making it **urgent** and **desirable** for managers to change their own behaviors. Though, I've noticed, I'm not the only one. Many management **teachers** experience the same thing. With techniques and games such as *Delegation Poker* [Appelo 2011b] and *Moving Motivators* [Appelo 2011c] I am trying to make it a little **easier** for people to be better managers. And by making such exercises available for download I allow people plenty of **practice**. Unfortunately, despite the fact that such exercises easily generate **short-term wins**, in many organizations it is very hard to make good management behaviors **sustainable**.

Stimulate the Network

I feel thrilled that, since I quit my job in October 2010, I am **fully committed** to the cause of organizational transformation. And, particularly since the gathering in Stoos, I know I'm not the only one, and I hope the many change agents are able to learn how to **assist each other**. Better management started with **innovators** such as Ricardo Semler (Semco), Bill Gore (W.L. Gore), Herb Kelleher (Southwest Airlines), John Mackey (Whole Foods) and Zhang Ruimin (Haier). Then there were **early adopters** (including authors and speakers) who picked up what the innovators were doing, and started broadcasting it to others using books, blogs, and conference talks. Now the question is how to get the **leaders** on our side, among which I would count MBA schools, management clubs, leadership institutes, and governments. They could all play a crucial role in order to reach the **early majority** of managers who are still managing the traditional way, but are willing to consider better alternatives. Certainly, it would be great if there was a way to enable modern management practices to **go viral**, but I have no idea how to do this. In the meantime, the late majority will start resisting, and I'm already keeping my eyes and ears open to learn from the **skeptics**. Fortunately, considering that we barely got started changing the world, the problem of a **relapse** is at least one issue we don't have to concern ourselves with yet.

Change the Environment

While I try to influence people, and think about the adoption curve of global change, I spend a lot of time writing, speaking, and thinking of other ways to **radiate information** about successful change. Behind the scenes I sometimes help conference organizers because such community events **ease communication** between people who otherwise find it difficult to exchange ideas. One topic I still struggle with is the **group**

identity of managers and the **peer pressure** of informal management networks that now sends many of them in the *wrong* direction. The commonly used **incentives** in management circles are also completely the opposite of how managers *should* be incentivized. (And I have yet to figure out if there really is something that we can do about this.) Finally, considering that physical **barriers** and **guides** don't seem to be applicable in this case, the world might need the help of some **institutions** to define social standards or rules of good conduct.

Well, that's *my* change management challenge. But enough about me…

Now It's Your Turn

What's *your* challenge?

How will *you* try to influence the people around you? Feel free to let me know. But don't forget to ask yourself the questions that were outlined in this booklet. I'm sure they can help you, at least a little, in your valiant effort to change the world.

Good luck!

Appendix A: Change Agent Game

There is a simple exercise available for change agents who want to practice their skills, or discuss their change initiatives with peers. The exercise can be downloaded from the following location:

http://www.management30.com/change-agent/

The exercise consists of the 34 questions listed in this book. The participants in the exercise are asked to tell each other stories of successful change, either from their own experience or elsewhere. They tell their stories based on the questions that they see in front of them.

What Makes It Sustainable?

People: Reinforcement

The sustainability of new behavior is best achieved when you can turn the boring parts of it into something that is fun. Can you anchor your new approach in people's minds by adding social, competitive, or other addictive dimensions, so that people want to keep on doing it?

How Do You Radiate Information?

Environment: Information

A crucial part of many change initiatives is to change the environment so that people better understand what's going on. How will you make sure that change can be seen by everyone? How will you make the invisible visible, and broadcast the need for change to everyone?

Download the exercise and check if you can be a great change agent!

Appendix B: Management 3.0 Book

Agile management is an often overlooked part of Agile. There are at least a hundred books for Agile developers and project managers, but very few for Agile managers and leaders.

However, when organizations adopt Agile software development, not only developers and project managers need to learn new practices. Development managers and team leaders must also learn a different approach to leading and managing organizations.

Several studies indicate that management is the biggest obstacle in transitions to Agile software development. Managers need to learn what their new role is in software development organizations in the 21st century, and how to get the best out of Agile. This book will help them.

An important portion of the book deals with complexity theory, and how ideas and concepts from this scientific field can be translated to management of software development teams. The book is half theory/half practice. It aims at managers who want to become Agile, and agilists who want to become managers.

Management 3.0: Leading Agile Developers, Developing Agile Leaders was written by Jurgen Appelo, and is published by Addison-Wesley in the Mike Cohn Signature Series.

http://www.management30.com/

Appendix C: Management 3.0 Course

Duration

2-day course

Target Audience

The Management 3.0 course aims at leaders/managers who want to become Agile, and people who want to become great team leaders or line managers. (No practical experience with Agile methods is necessary, though some familiarity with Agile principles and practices is useful.)

The course typically draws team leaders (15%), development managers (15%), agile coaches (15%), scrum masters (15%), project managers (10%), product owners (10%), developers and testers (10%), and top-level management (10%).

Topics

- Agile Development
- Complexity Thinking
- Energize People
- Empower Teams
- Align Constraints
- Develop Competence
- Grow Structure
- Improve Everything

Games and Exercises

Each of the eight topics includes at least one game or exercise where people put into practice the ideas of the course in groups of five or six people. Sometimes the attendees play as different managers against each other. Sometimes they act together as one manager, sharing their thoughts while working on a problem.

Every exercise ends with a debrief and a discussion, so that people can relate what they've learned to their own situation, and bring up questions and experiences to be addressed by the whole group.

Course Schedule

http://www.management30.com/course-schedule/

Appendix D: Stoos Network

Reflecting on leadership in organizations today, we find ourselves in a bit of a mess. We see reliance on linear, mechanistic thinking, companies focusing more on stock price than delighting customers, and knowledge workers whose voices are ignored by the bosses who direct them. All these factors are reflected in the current economic crisis, increased inequity, bankruptcies, and widespread disillusionment.

There has to be a better way.

In January 2012, a diverse group of 21 people including senior executives, business strategists, managers, academics, and lean-agile development practitioners from four continents met in Stoos, Switzerland. We believe that we uncovered some of the common characteristics of that better way. For example,

> "Organizations can become learning networks of individuals creating value and that the role of leaders should include the stewardship of the living rather than the management of the machine.

Most importantly, we committed to continue our work, both in person and online. A problem this size will require many minds and hearts. We'd love to hear your voice and your experience. Help move the conversation forward by joining our LinkedIn group and on Twitter with hashtag #stoos.

Let's start the transformation, before it's too late.

http://www.stoosnetwork.org/

Appendix E: Agile Lean Europe Network

The Agile Lean Europe (ALE) network is an open and evolving network of people (not businesses), with links to local communities and institutes.

It helps people in European countries by spreading ideas and growing a collective memory of Agile and Lean thinking.

And by exchanging interesting people with diverse perspectives across borders it allows beautiful results to emerge.

> "ALE is a network for collaboration of Agile & Lean thinkers and activists across Europe.

http://alenetwork.eu/

Bibliography

Appelo, Jurgen. *Management 3.0: Leading Agile Developers, Developing Agile Leaders*. Upper Saddle River, NJ: Addison-Wesley, 2011 (a).

Appelo, Jurgen. "Delegation Poker (Game Description)" *NOOP.NL* <http://bit.ly/erABUk> March 15, 2011 (b).

Appelo, Jurgen. "Moving Motivators (Free Exercise)" *NOOP.NL* <http://bit.ly/omffNN> September 26, 2011 (c).

Appelo, Jurgen. "The Happiness Door, Another Great Feedback Method" *NOOP.NL* <http://bit.ly/s5HSD6> November 13, 2011 (d).

Appelo, Jurgen. "New Group - Agile Lean Europe (ALE)" *NOOP.NL* <http://bit.ly/fkM6Uo> February 15, 2011 (e).

Bobinski, Dan. "Performance Appraisals Don't Work" *Management-Issues.com* <http://bit.ly/cEAgPH> July 8, 2010.

Bowman, Sharon. *Training from the Back of the Room!*. San Diego: Pfeiffer, 2009.

Burke, W. Warner. *Organization Change: Theory and Practice*. Thousand Oaks: SAGE Publications, 2010.

Covey, Stephen. *The 7 Habits of Highly Effective People: Restoring the Character Ethic*. New York: Free Press, 2004.

Deci, Edward L. and Richard M. Ryan. *Handbook of Self-determination Research*. Rochester, NY: University of Rochester Press, 2002.

Deming, W. Edwards. *Out of the Crisis*. Cambridge: Massachusetts Institute of Technology, 1986.

Denning, Stephen, "The Shift Index 2011: The Most Important Business Study Ever? " *Forbes* <http://onforb.es/yLkxul> January 25, 2012 (a)

Denning, Stephen, "HBR Blows The Lid Off C-Suite Over-Compensation" *Forbes* <http://onforb.es/y23vPk> February 22, 2012 (b)

Drucker, Peter F. *Management*. London: Collins, 1974.

Fleming, Nic. "The Bonus Myth: How Paying for Results Can Backfire" *NewScientist* <http://bit.ly/fK7uXJ> April 12, 2011.

Gladwell, Malcolm. *The Tipping Point*. Boston: Little, Brown, 2000.

Goetz, Thomas. "Harnessing the Power of Feedback Loops" *Wired* <http://bit.ly/loX33y> June 19, 2011.

Heath, Chip and Dan Heath. *Made to Stick: Why Some Ideas Survive and Others Die*. New York: Random House, 2007.

Heath, Chip and Dan Heath. *Switch: How to Change Things When Change is Hard*. New York: Broadway Books, 2010.

Hiatt, Jeff. *ADKAR: A Model for Change in Business, Government, and Our Community*. Loveland, Colorado: Prosci Learning Center Publications, 2006.

Jackson, Michael. *Systems Thinking: Creative Holism for Managers*. Chichester, West Sussex Hoboken, N.J: John Wiley & Sons, 2003.

Jensen, Eric. *Enriching the Brain*. San Francisco: Jossey-Bass, A John Wiley & Sons Imprint, 2006.

Kotter, John. *Leading Change*. Boston, Mass: Harvard Business School Press, 1996.

Manns, Mary Lynn & Linda Rising. *Fearless Change: Patterns for Introducing New Ideas*. Boston: Addison-Wesley, 2005.

Meadows, Donella. *Thinking in Systems: A Primer*. White River Junction, Vt: Chelsea Green Pub, 2008.

Medina, John. *Brain Rules*. City: Pear Press, 2008.

Mitchell, Melanie. *Complexity*. City: Oxford U Pr, N Y, 2009.

Moore, Geoffrey. *Crossing the Chasm: Marketing and Selling Disruptive Products to Mainstream Customers*. New York, NY: HarperBusiness Essentials, 2002.

Patterson, Kerry, et al. *Influencer: The Power to Change Anything*. New York: McGraw-Hill, 2008.

Pink, Daniel. Drive: *The Surprising Truth about What Motivates Us*. New York, NY: Riverhead Books, 2009.

Pulford, Kevin et.al. *A Quantitative Approach to Software Management*. San Francisco: Ignatius Press, 1996.

Reiss, Steven. *Who Am I?: The 16 Basic Desires That Motivate Our Behavior and Define Our Personality*. New York: Berkley Pub, 2002.

Ries, Eric. *The Lean Startup*. New York: Crown Business, 2011.

Rogers, Everett M. *Diffusion of Innovations: 5th Edition*. New York: Free Press, 2003.

Saddington, Peter. "Top 200 Agile Blogs" *Agile Scout* <http://bit.ly/jQHfRM> June 6, 2011.

Senge, Peter. *The Fifth Discipline: The Art and Practice of the Learning Organization*. New York: Doubleday/Currency, 2006.

Thiagarajan, Sivasailam. *Thiagi's 100 Favorite Games*. San Diego: Pfeiffer, 2006.

Van Vugt, Mark. "Triumph of the Commons: Helping the World to Share" *NewScientist* <http://bit.ly/p9ULM> August 25, 2009.

http://www.facebook.com/Management30

http://www.linkedin.com/groups/Management-30-4074448

http://plus.google.com/u/0/117055317275223396630

http://twitter.com/management30

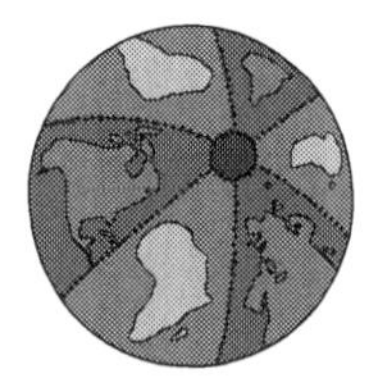

http://www.management30.com/how-to-change-the-world

Made in the USA
Lexington, KY
06 March 2014